Creatures of the Forest Habitat

Foxes

David Lee

PowerKiDS press.
New York

Published in 2017 by The Rosen Publishing Group, Inc.
29 East 21st Street, New York, NY 10010

First Edition

Editor: Caitie McAneney
Book Design: Mickey Harmon

Photo Credits: Cover (series logo) iLoveCoffeeDesign/Shutterstock.com; cover, pp. 1, 3, 4, 6, 8, 10, 12, 14, 16, 18, 20, 22–24 (background) BlueRingMedia/Shutterstock.com; cover (fox) Jun Su/Shutterstock.com; p. 5 (red fox) Kristo Robert/Shutterstock.com; p. 5 (fennec fox) Chris Humphries/Shutterstock.com; p. 5 (Arctic fox) Erni/Shutterstock.com; p. 7 (Arctic fox) Josef Pittner/Shutterstock.com; p. 7 (kit fox) Brad Sauter/Shutterstock.com; p. 7 (gray fox) Holly Kuchera/Shutterstock.com; p. 9 Steve Oehlenschlager/Shutterstock.com; p. 11 Menno Schaefer/Shutterstock.com; p. 13 Miroslav Hlavko/Shutterstock.com; p. 14 Yanik Chauvin/Shutterstock.com; p. 15 Studiotouch/Shutterstock.com; p. 17 (main) Wesley Aston/Shutterstock.com; p. 17 (bird) Rainer Fuhrmann/Shutterstock.com; p. 17 (mouse) Rudmer Zwerver/Shutterstock.com; p. 17 (frog) Preobrajenskiy/Shutterstock.com; p. 19 (inset) Clea Calderoni/Shutterstock.com; p. 19 (main) Jamie Hall/Shutterstock.com; p. 21 Andrew M. Allport/Shutterstock.com; p. 22 Eric Isselee/Shutterstock.com.

Cataloging-in-Publication Data
Names: Lee, David.
Title: Foxes / David Lee.
Description: New York : PowerKids Press, 2017. | Series: Creatures of the forest habitat | Includes index.
Identifiers: ISBN 9781499427127 (pbk.) | ISBN 9781499429299 (library bound) | ISBN 9781499427134 (6 pack)
Subjects: LCSH: Foxes–Juvenile literature.
Classification: LCC QL737.C22 L44 2017 | DDC 599.775–dc23

Manufactured in the United States of America

CPSIA Compliance Information: Batch #BW17PK: For Further Information contact Rosen Publishing, New York, New York at 1-800-237-9932

Contents

Foxes in the Forest

Forests are important **habitats** for many animals. One of the most common forest animals is the fox. There are more than 30 species, or kinds, of foxes in the world, and many of them call a forest home.

Foxes are part of the Canidae family, which includes dogs and wolves. They even look a little like dogs. There are a dozen species of "true" foxes. They include the red fox, fennec fox, Arctic fox, and kit fox.

Forest Friend Facts

The red fox is the largest fox species in the world.

fennec fox

Arctic fox

red fox

This red fox hides behind the branches and leaves of the forest's trees.

Finding a Fox

Where can you find a fox? Foxes live throughout much of the world. They live in North America, South America, Europe, Asia, Africa, and Australia.

The red fox has the widest **range** of any animal in the Canidae family. Its range stretches from the warm **regions** of Central America to the cold Arctic Circle. It also lives in North Africa and central Asia. The gray fox is found from Canada to the South American countries of Venezuela and Colombia.

Forest Friend Facts

The gray fox lives in many regions of the southwestern United States.

Other foxes found in North America include the Arctic fox and the kit fox.

At Home in the Forest

The forest is a great place for many foxes to live. They can use the trees for shelter and for **stalking** their **prey**. They can make their dens in caves or hollowed-out logs. Red foxes like to live in the forest. They also live in mountains and grasslands.

Not all foxes live in the forest. Arctic foxes live in the Arctic tundra, which is a very cold land with no trees. The kit fox lives in the deserts of the southwestern United States and Mexico.

Forest Friend Facts

The fennec fox doesn't live in a forest. This fox lives in the Sahara Desert in North Africa. Its big ears help keep the fox cool in the hot desert.

Red foxes like to dig underground dens to live in.

Fox Features

How can you identify a fox if you see one in the forest? Look at its features. Most foxes are about the size of a medium-sized dog.

Red foxes often have an orange or reddish coat of fur. They have a very bushy tail, which is sometimes called a brush. Red foxes use this tail for warmth when it's cold outside. The tail has a white tip. Red foxes have black feet and ear tips and a white belly and chest.

Forest Friend Facts

The fennec fox is the smallest fox species in the world. It only grows to about the size of a cat!

A fox's tail helps it balance. This helps the red fox climb trees in the forest!

A Red Fox's Life

Adult red foxes often live and hunt alone. That makes them solitary animals. However, male and female foxes come together in the winter to **mate**. Then, the female fox gives birth to a litter of baby foxes, which are called pups or kits. Each mother red fox has about two to 12 pups at once.

A red fox family sticks together during the first summer. Fox parents teach pups how to hunt and find food. In the fall, the pups are ready to live and hunt on their own.

Forest Friend Facts

Female foxes are called vixens and male foxes are called tods or dog foxes.

Pups are usually gray or brown when they're born. They are also blind and deaf for a couple of weeks. They need their parents to survive.

Fox Behaviors

Foxes are thought to be smart and wise. There are many **legends** about this forest animal. What are foxes really like?

Foxes are very **flexible** about their habitats and what they'll eat. They're good at adapting, or changing to fit their surroundings. They're often alone, but they know how to communicate with one another. A fox may move its tail in a certain way to signal to other foxes. It may also mark a tree or rock with its waste to claim **territory**.

Forest Friend Facts

Foxes are most active at night, which makes them nocturnal. Some are active during the day, especially foxes that live near neighborhoods.

Young foxes love to play and wrestle with each other.

Favorite Foods

Foxes are omnivores. That means they eat both meat and plants. Foxes will eat many different kinds of food, which helps them adapt to new places.

Foxes are great hunters. They have sharp teeth, and they can leap very high to land on their prey. Foxes often eat small animals, such as rabbits and mice. They will also eat frogs, birds, and **carrion**. Foxes that live near farms sometimes eat small farm animals, such as chickens. They also eat fruits and vegetables.

Forest Friend Facts

Red foxes will eat pet food and trash if they live around people.

This red fox tucks its front legs into its body and leaps high in the air to hunt mice.

mice

frogs

birds

Foxes and People

Foxes are often considered pests, or unwanted animals, when they move into neighborhoods or near farms. Because they'll eat anything, they sometimes get into trash or attack farm animals.

Sometimes foxes will come up to people. If they do, they're probably used to people feeding them. However, it's easy to scare them by making a loud noise. They will usually run away. Foxes are only a danger to people if they have rabies. Rabies is a deadly illness that's usually spread through animal bites.

If you know foxes live nearby, keep your pets indoors at night. Foxes normally don't hurt people, but they may get into a fight with a pet.

Foxes at Risk

Foxes only live for around two or three years in the wild. One of the greatest **threats** to them is being hunted by humans. People hunt some fox species, such as red foxes and Arctic foxes, for their fur. The fur is then used to make clothing.

Other people hunt foxes for sport. In England, fox hunting has been a popular sport since the 1400s. People use dogs to chase a fox while they follow on horseback. If the fox is caught, it is killed.

Forest Friend Facts

Fox hunting was banned in England and Wales in 2005. However, types of fox hunts still take place.

Farmers may kill or trap foxes that come onto their farm.

Keeping the Forest Safe

One of the biggest threats to all forest animals, including foxes, is deforestation. Deforestation is when people cut down too many trees in a forest habitat. People cut down trees to make room for farms and ranches. People use trees to make homes, furniture, and many other products. This forces all the forest animals to leave their homes.

Luckily, foxes adapt well to new places. They can live in rocky habitats, dry habitats, and grassy habitats. They'll even live in neighborhoods. However, it's important to keep our forests safe so foxes can live in their natural homes!

Glossary

carrion: A dead, rotting animal.

flexible: Willing to change or try different things.

habitat: The natural place where an animal or plant lives.

legend: A story handed down from the past.

mate: To come together to make babies.

prey: An animal hunted by other animals for food.

range: The area where something lives.

region: A large area of land that has a number of features in common.

stalk: To hunt slowly and quietly.

territory: An area of land that an animal considers to be its own and will fight to defend.

threat: Something likely to cause harm.

Index

Websites

Due to the changing nature of Internet links, PowerKids Press has developed an online list of websites related to the subject of this book. This site is updated regularly. Please use this link to access the list: www.powerkidslinks.com/forest/fox